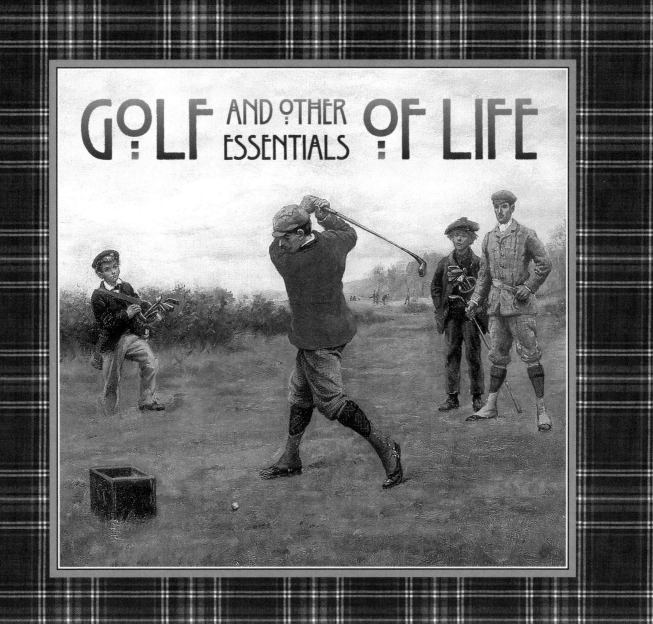

GOLF AND OTHER ESSENTIALS OF LIFE

TO MY SON ANDREW

The words *Andrew* and *Golf* have been closely linked together for over 500 years. May they continue to be so as you live out the spirit of the game as a son, husband and father, in life as in golf.

St. Andrews
the home
of Golf

FOREWORD

While all avid players would agree that golf is an essential element of life, most of them would acknowledge that there are other elements as well, that man cannot live by golf alone.

Frequently compared before, the lessons of golf and life have much in common. The game not only rewards us as a pastime, but has much to share if we will learn.

This inspirational classic, devoted to golf's glorious heritage, celebrates the ancient game and other abiding essentials for living life as it was meant to be. In golf as in life, we get out of it what we put into it.

The Editors

ILLUSTRATION CREDITS

Brownlow Private Collection: 2, 5, 6, 8, 9, 16, 17, 18, 20, 21, 22, 27, 32, 35, 36

Hobbs Golf Collection: 19, 30, 37 and assorted golf clubs and balls used throughout

Koechel Peterson & Associates: 12, 24, 42

Ralph Miller Golf Library: 13, 15, 23, 40, 43

Byron and Peggy Nelson: 46

Stock Montage, Inc.: 26

Wood River Gallery: Cover, 3, 10, 11, 14, 25, 29, 31, 33, 39, 41, 44, 45, 48

TEXT CREDITS

Bobby Jones' essay (Friendship, page 12) used by permission from *St. Andrews & Golf*, 1995, Market Street Press, Cincinnati, Ohio.

Byron Nelson's essay (Four Drivers Too Many, page 15) used by permission from Byron and Peggy Nelson, copyright 1993.

GOLF AND OTHER ESSENTIALS OF LIFE

Brownlow

A GAME FOR LIFE

Of the origin and history of this game little need be said. The term "golf," pronounced *goff*, is evidently derived from the German word *kolbe*, signifying a club, or the Dutch word *kolf*, of similar meaning, and implying a game which is played with club and ball. Games with club and ball are numerous, and their origin dates back to early man.

As far as Britain is concerned, the origin of golf must be conceded to Scotland. As early as March, 1457, the game was being played with such zeal as greatly to interfere with what was deemed a more popular necessity, that of training in archery. Although decrees were passed that golf "be cryit doun and nocht usit," and that "no place be used for futeball, golfe, or other sik unprofitabill sportes," the people gave no heed. Somehow they had become possessed of so fascinating a sport, that it further became necessary "to prohibit such pastymes as golf upon the Sabbath day." It may be the people were more amenable to this last decree, but nothing could dislodge the love and delight which the people of Scotland have always entertained for this their favourite game. In the end, it was recognized as the national game of Scotland and monarchs became not only its patrons, but also distinguished players.

As a lover of golf, I am constrained to say I think no man is more to be pitied than he who has not yet learned to play the game. And I can truthfully assert that few, if any, who have once learned the game will give it up unless physically compelled to do so. No saying is more true than, "once a golfer, always a golfer."

My object, however, is not merely to incite a love for the game. I desire also to mention some of its many advantages.

Golf became the national game of Scotland and monarchs became not only its patrons, but also distinguished players.

To play the game successfully requires a vast amount of most prompt and careful judgment. Like the face of nature, the game is a series of perpetual changes. Problem after problem or, if you like, difficulty after difficulty arises which you are called upon to surmount by cool judgment and prompt action. And as those same difficulties may never occur twice under similar circumstances, the exercise of judgment is demanding.

ONCE A GOLFER, ALWAYS A GOLFER

Another great advantage which golf possesses is that it can be played, and indeed is played, all the year 'round. It is possible with red balls to play it in snow, which I may say from personal experience adds considerably to the already invigorating exercise of walking, thinking, and striking.

Not only can golf be played all the year 'round, it may also be played from the cradle to the tomb. A child cannot begin too early. Although children and old men are physically unable to play a good game, or a game in full, still they may enjoy themselves almost equally as much as the stronger athlete.

Golf, then, is a game admirably adapted for almost all conditions of men. It results in the formation of friendly societies, such as gentlemen's clubs, artisans' clubs, caddies' clubs, and in seaside places there are also fishermen's clubs. All these, as a rule, meet and play on the same green without any collision whatever because all submit to the strict discipline of the game. Indeed, a golf rule commands more respect and prompt obedience than do many of the Ten Commandments.

Another great advantage connected with golf is that as a rule you can always choose your own partner. But sometimes in match play you may become paired with a stranger. However, in that stranger you may discover one whose further acquaintance would be agreeable to you. In this sense golf is a means of making friends by a more agreeable method than most games possess. At the risk of being condemned for an error of judgment, I am inclined to regard golf as the most sociable of all outdoor games. The companion of a day sometimes becomes the friend of a lifetime. And it is no uncommon thing for golfers thus allied in friendship to indulge in a golfing tour. Now can anything more desirable than this be conceived?

W. T. Linskill
Founder and Captain
Cambridge University Golf Club

Medal Day,
St. Andrews

They say golf is like life but don't believe them. Golf is more complicated than that.
Gardner Dickinson

THE ANCIENT ART OF PUTTING

Walter Travis did not begin playing golf until age 35, but was the most feared amateur of his day because of his incomparable putting. In 1904 he won the British Amateur Championship using the new center-shafted Schenectady putter which he borrowed from a friend the day before. The putter was banned for a time in Britain, making Travis an even bigger hero back home.

It is a matter of common knowledge that I have experimented with more kinds of putters than any other player in this country, and should therefore be expected to have at least learned what not to do.

I have tried wooden putters, gun-metal putters, straight-faced putters, cylindrical putters, mallet-headed putters, putting cleeks, cleeks, left-handed putting cleeks—in short, the whole family of every conceivable kind of weapon that human ingenuity has evolved for the purpose. I have tried them all in every imaginable position.

The sum of all my experience shows conclusively that the really good putter is largely born, not made. He is inherently endowed with a good eye and a tactile delicacy of grip which are denied the ordinary run of mortals. However less favored players may, by the adoption of methods which have stood the test of actual experience, significantly improve their game.

Putting is largely mental, and on this account becomes so difficult. The novice, who has no recollections of scores of missed putts a couple of feet or so from the hole, is more apt to bring off a putt of this distance than the other fellow. He is not troubled with any thought of being a yard or more away on a miss, and in blissful ignorance confidently bangs away and holes.

There are putters and putters. If a man putts poorly it isn't so much the fault of the club as of the putter. A naturally good putter will putt fairly well with any old weapon. At the same time, I am of the opinion that the best results can be secured by a putting cleek with a short shaft.

> *Walter J. Travis*
> U.S. Amateur Champion 1900, 1901, 1903
> British Amateur Champion 1904

Ninety percent of the putts that fall short don't go in.

> *Yogi Berra*

Why am I using a new putter?
Because the old one didn't float too well.

> *Craig Stadler*, 1993 U.S. Open

Never break your putter and your driver in the same round or you're dead.

> *Tommy Bolt*

Every shot counts. The three-foot putt is just as important as the 300-yard drive.

> *Henry Cotton*

Love and putting are mysteries for the philosopher to solve. Both subjects are beyond golfers.

> *Tommy Armour*

Ben Hogan's wife, Valerie, accompanied him on his tours. One night she was watching him practice putting in their hotel room. After sitting patiently for some time, she offered him a bit of advice, "All you have to do is hit the ball closer to the hole," she said.

The big trick in putting is not method—the secret of putting is domination of the nerves.
Henry Cotton

I'm having putting troubles. But it's not the putter, it's the puttee.
Frank Beard

DEVELOP YOUR OWN STYLE

I have told you repeatedly that you must develop your own style, and while I have described some of my own methods, I repeat that you must not necessarily follow them except in general principle. By this time you may know sufficient about the game to be able to make experiments for yourself. Try to form your own style, remembering that it is the work you do yourself that will help you to become a good golfer. Hints and tips from others may be useful at times, but more often than not these work only for a few days. If you work out your own game on the lines I have suggested you will soon discover for yourself what is useful to you and what not. But it is only hard work—disheartening work, sometimes—that can make you the player you would wish to be.

T. H. COTTON

Henry Cotten
"Redeemer of British Golf"
British Open Champion 1934, 1937, 1948

There is no gold mine so rich in possibilities as your own experience. Buried in your memory, ready to be dug out, evaluated and applied to present problems, is a record of all your mistakes and failures, all your triumphs and successes. You have only to select what you feel will be of aid to you in the form of some wisdom or judgment or skill you have gained through some past experience—and you have a power at hand to serve your current need. The most successful men and women are those who have learned how to make the best use of the talents and knowledge acquired throughout life.

Harold Sherman

To be nobody but yourself—in a world which is doing its best, night and day, to make you everybody else—means to fight the hardest battle which any human being can fight, and never stop fighting.

e. e. cummings

Learn to think for yourself. You are not everybody's dog that whistles.

Early American Proverb

Neglect not the gift that is in thee.

1 Timothy 4:14

Be yourself. Who else is better qualified?

Frank J. Giblin II

Each of us, every human being in the world, is distinct. That raw stuff of our unique selfhood is our most precious possession. But how easily it gets buffeted and crushed by what other people think, by the herd spirit, by the stereotype into which custom and prejudice try to fit us. We need quiet to keep in touch with ourselves, to recharge the soul that is uniquely ours. You need quiet to just be you, rather than a straw man.

L. R. Ditzen

KEEPING HOPE ALIVE

G olf is not one of those occupations in which you soon learn your level. There is no shape nor size of body, no awkwardness nor ungainliness, which puts good golf beyond one's reach. There are good golfers with spectacles, with one eye, with one leg, even with one arm. None but the absolutely blind need despair. It is not the youth alone who has cause to hope. Beginners in middle age have become great, and, more wonderful still, after years of patient duffering, there may be a rift in the clouds. Some pet vice which has been clung to as a virtue may be abandoned, and the fifth-class player burst upon the world as a medal winner. In golf, whilst there is life there is hope.

Sir Walter Simpson

A prime function for a leader is to keep hope alive.

Anonymous

Hope, like faith, is nothing if it is not courageous: it is nothing if it is not ridiculous.

Thornton Wilder

May your unfailing love rest upon us, O Lord, even as we put our hope in you.

Psalm 33:22

There is no medicine like hope, no incentive so great, and no tonic so powerful as expectation of something tomorrow.

O. S. Marden

Good memories are sweet and bad ones are destructive. But whatever the case, sooner or later, the past must be left behind and we must focus on the present and the future. As Chi Chi Rodriguez says, "The sweetest two words in the world are 'next time.'"

A Scottish lad learning the game

If you really want to get better at golf, go back and take it up at a much earlier age.
Anonymous

Everything that is done in the world is done by hope.
Martin Luther

GOLF IN NORTH AMERICA

While the earliest recorded golf clubs were formed in Montreal in 1873, Quebec in 1874, and in Toronto in 1876, golf was played much earlier in Virginia, South Carolina, and Maryland.

According to port records in 1743, David Deas of Charleston, South Carolina, ordered 96 golf clubs and 432 balls from Leith, Scotland. Deas grew up in Scotland playing golf, and after coming to America, imported the game as well. From 1743 to 1765, records reveal that a total of at least 186 golf clubs and nearly 1,200 golf balls arrived in America to fuel the growth of the Scottish passion in the southern United States.

Golf is a wonderful game. It is more than a game to me; it is a life's work, a career, a profession. Whether it is a science or an art I do not know. It is probably half and half, but it is a noble occupation all the same.

Henry Cotten

Had the Civil War not dramatically changed the life and leisure of Southern aristocrats, golf clubs would certainly have emerged. However, the first golf clubs began in Canada, as previously mentioned, and were quickly followed by the first American club in Yonkers, New York, in 1888.

On Washington's birthday, February 22, 1888, six men gathered in a cow pasture in Yonkers to experiment with the new clubs and gutta-percha balls. Two of the six men, Robert Lockhart and John Reid, were Scottish school-mates. Lockhart returned regularly to St. Andrews on business and soon discovered the shop of Old Tom Morris. He purchased the handmade clubs and balls, bringing them back without any realization of what he was beginning. As a result of the instant popularity of the game, the St. Andrew's Golf Club of Yonkers began.

Soon the club had 13 members and relocated the course from the cow pasture to an apple orchard four blocks north. One particular apple tree near the first tee and final green served as clubhouse and 19th hole. As a result the players came to be known as "The Apple Tree Gang."

Other golf clubs soon began springing up independently. Shinnecock Hills Golf Club opened in 1891 with the first real American golf course designed for the purpose. By the next year, they also boasted of an imposing structure that was America's first golf clubhouse. In 1894, over a dinner in New York City, the United States Golf Association (USGA) was created to supervise and regulate the growing phenomenon. The five influential clubs that created the USGA were: (1) St. Andrew's of Yonkers; (2) Newport, Rhode Island; (3) Shinnecock Hills, Long Island; (4) The Country Club of Brookline, Massachusetts; and (5) the Chicago Golf Club.

FRIENDS OF THE GAME

Having won the Open (1927) and the Amateur (1930) on the Old Course, Bobby Jones returned to St. Andrews for the last time in 1958. At that time, the city honored him with an award that only one other American, Benjamin Franklin 200 years earlier, had ever received. Jones had captured their hearts, as well as their titles, like no other foreigner because of his flair for golf and the strength of his character.

That evening, the hall was full and Bobby (now crippled by a spinal disease) made his way to the podium to accept the award. Without notes and speaking from the heart, Jones concluded the emotional remarks by describing his thoughts on friendship:

> *Friends are a man's priceless treasures, and a life rich in friendship is full indeed. When I say, with due regard for the meaning of the word, that I am your friend, I have pledged to you the ultimate in loyalty and devotion. In some respects friendship may even transcend love, for in true friendship there is no place for jealousy. When I say that you are my friends, it is possible that I am imposing upon you a greater burden than you are willing to assume. But when you have made me aware on many occasions that you have a kindly feeling toward me, and when you have honored me by every means at your command, then when I call you friend, I am at once affirming my high regard and affection for you and declaring my complete faith in you and trust in the sincerity of your expressions.*

For those in attendance, it was a night of tears and memories never to be forgotten.

Be slow in choosing a friend, slower in changing.

Benjamin Franklin

In golf there are no strangers,
but only friends you've never met.

Bill Campbell

My best friend is the one who brings out the best in me.

Henry Ford

Listening is a magnetic and strange thing, a creative force. The friends who listen to us are the ones we move toward, and we want to sit in their radius. When we are listened to, it creates us, makes us unfold and expand.

Karl Menninger

Be courteous to all, but intimate with few, and let those few be well tried before you give them your confidence. True friendship is a plant of slow growth and must undergo and withstand the shocks of adversity.

George Washington

Friendships form among people who strengthen one another.

Franklin Owen

The thing that counts most in pursuit of happiness is choosing the right traveling companion.

Anonymous

Don't praise your own good shots.
Leave that function to your partner who,
if a good sport, will not be slow in performing it.

Harry Vardon

God evidently does not intend us all to be rich, or powerful, or great, but he does intend us all to be friends.

Ralph Waldo Emerson

The firmest friendships have been formed in mutual adversity, as iron is most strongly united by the fiercest flame.

Charles Colton

True friends don't sympathize with your weakness— they help summon your strength.

Anonymous

Two are better than one, because they have a good return for their work: If one falls down, his friend can help him up. But pity the man who falls and has no one to help him up!

Ecclesiastes 4:9-10

Five years from now you will be pretty much the same as you are today except for two things: the books you read and the people you get close to.

Charles Jones

Bobby Jones, Jess Sweetser, Gene Sarazen and Walter Hagen at the end of their 36-hole benefit match on the links of the New York Athletic Club, October 27, 1923

Never needle, harass or poke fun at a playing partner who's on the edge of despair.

Doug Sanders

When I think of those who have influenced my life the most, I think not of the great but of the good.

John Knox

In choosing a partner, always pick the optimist.

Tony Lema

FOUR DRIVERS TOO MANY

Byron Nelson handcrafted a new style of driver the day before the 1935 U.S. Open at Oakmont. As amazing as that may be, the story of why he did it is even more so.

When I got home the first night after we got there, I'd just finished my first practice round, and hadn't been driving the ball as well as I thought I should. Not that the rest of my game was flawless—far from it. But my driving was the most inconsistent of all. In the past year, I'd bought four drivers and probably spent more than I should have, since money was very scarce right then. In fact, we were so poor we were staying in the basement of a parsonage while I played in the Open, so you know we weren't doing too well financially.

Anyway, that evening, I sat with Louise after dinner and thought about my driving, while she did some needlework. Finally I said, "Louise, I need to buy another driver. I'm driving terrible." There wasn't any reaction for a couple of minutes. Then she put her work down and said, "Byron, we've been married over a year. I haven't bought a new dress or a new pair of shoes or anything for myself in all that time. But you've bought four new drivers, and you're not happy with any of them. One of two things—either you don't know what kind of driver you want, or you don't know how to drive."

Well, that stopped me in my tracks. Because there was no denying what she'd said was right. So the next morning, early, I took one of the drivers I had, a Spalding, to the shop there at Oakmont as soon as they opened, and went to work. Dutch Loeffler, the pro there for many years, was very kind and let me use whatever I needed.

Nearly all the drivers then were made with a completely straight face— same as when they had hickory shafts. That straight face worked all right when you pronated and didn't use your lower body at all, but with the steel shafts, it was very unsatisfactory. Now, I'd had in my mind for quite a while what a driver should really look

Byron at the 1937 British Open at Carnoustie, Scotland

like. So I began shaving off, very, very gradually, a slight bit off the toe of the club, then the heel, and kept that up till it had a nice little rounded face—what's called a "bulge." When I got it to looking exactly like that picture in my mind, I smoothed it off, put the finish on, and went out to play. And I never had any trouble with my driving after that, even though I didn't score very well in that particular Open.

Eventually, when I went to work for MacGregor, I had Kuzzy Kustenborder, head of their custom-made club department, make me a persimmon driver to those specifications, and that was the driver I used from 1940 throughout the rest of my career. It's now in the World Golf Hall of Fame. Today, Roger Cleveland of Cleveland Golf Company makes a driver with my name on it that's an exact copy of the one I used to win nearly all my tournaments. But I guess I might still be looking for the perfect driver if it hadn't been for what Louise said to me back in 1935.

Byron Nelson

THE PATRIARCH OF GOLF

Old Tom Morris and his son, Young Tom, dominated the world of golf for only about a decade by their masterful play, but they have dominated it ever since by their status as legends.

Old Tom was born and trained at St. Andrews. Upon hearing a friend haphazardly ask why Tom did not become an apprentice to the great golfer and clubmaker, Allan Robertson, Tom did just that. He later would win the Open

Old Tom Morris, the most photographed and painted golfer of his day, played in every Open Championship from 1860 to 1896. He was a clubmaster, ballmaker, caddie, course designer, greenkeeper, and four-time Open Champion.

(there was only one Open at the time—the British) in 1861, 1862, 1864, and 1867, with all four victories coming at Prestwick. At the age of 17, Young Tom took over the family business of winning Opens by taking the title three years in a row from 1868 to 1870. From Old Tom's shop across from the 18th green, he was a clubmaker, golf course designer, and teacher of the game. Even after the age of 60, Tom displayed an extraordinarily fine game, winning two professional matches and playing St. Andrews in 1881 on his 64th birthday.

Most of us would think that golf consumed his entire life. But Tom Morris was more than a golfer. After his death, his friends and fellow believers at Holy Trinity Church in St. Andrews placed this marble epitaph on a prominent inside wall of the church. It testifies for all to see that Tom knew there was more to life than golf:

> TO THE MEMORY OF TOM MORRIS.
> BORN 16 JUNE 1821, DIED 24 MAY 1908:
> AN ELDER FOR 18 YEARS IN THE PARISH;
> COURTEOUS, KINDLY, UPRIGHT, DEVOUT,
> GENEROUS IN RIVALRY, MODEST IN VICTORY,
> HE WAS BELOVED AND HONOURED
> BY FRIENDS OF ALL RANKS.
>
> *Holy Trinity Church,*
> *St. Andrews, Scotland*

He was golf's great patriarch as the game entered the 20th century—a century of explosive growth and worldwide affection. Never was the game in better hands than those of Old Tom Morris.

A TEST OF CHARACTER

Golf is a test of temper, a trial of honour, a revealer of character. It affords a chance to play the man and act the gentleman. It means going out into God's out-of-doors, getting close to nature, fresh air, exercise, a sweeping away of the mental cobwebs, and genuine recreation. It is a cure for care—an antidote to worry. It includes companionship with friends, social interaction, opportunities for courtesy, kindliness and generosity to an opponent. It promotes not only physical health but moral force.

David Robertson Forgan, 1898

The only way of really finding out a man's true character is to play golf with him. In no other walk of life does the cloven hoof so quickly display itself.

P. G. Wodehouse

The Lord detests a perverse man but takes the upright into his confidence.

Proverbs 3:32

Golf puts a man's character on the anvil and his richest qualities—patience, poise, restraint—to the flame.

Billy Casper

Reputation is what folks think you are. Personality is what you seem to be. Character is what you really are.

Anonymous

Like one's own children, golf has an uncanny way of endearing itself to us while at the same time evoking every weakness of mind and character, no matter how well hidden.

W. Timothy Gallwey

You can tell a lot about a person, even a total stranger, by playing a round of golf with him.

John Freeman

Sports do not build character. They reveal it.

Heywood Broun

One cannot always be a hero, but one can always be a man.

Johann Wolfgang von Goethe

Character is something each one of us must build for himself, out of the laws of God and nature, the examples of others, and—most of all—out of the trials and errors of daily life. Character is the total of thousands of small daily strivings to live up to the best that is in us.

Lt. Gen. A. G. Trudeau

Fame is a vapor, popularity an accident, riches take wings, those who cheer today will curse tomorrow, only one thing endures—character.

Horace Greeley

We speak of eyeball-to-eyeball encounters between men great and small. Even more searching and revealing of character is the eyeball-to-golfball confrontation, whereby our most secret natures are mercilessly tested by a small, round, whitish object with no mind or will but with a very definite life of its own, and with whims perverse and beatific.

John Stuart Martin

Golf is a game of integrity.
Raymond Floyd

What lies behind us and what lies before us are tiny matters compared to what lies within us.
Ralph Waldo Emerson

THE BUNKERS OF GOLF & LIFE

Bunkers, if they are good bunkers, and bunkers of strong character, refuse to be disregarded and insist on asserting themselves. They do not mind being avoided, but they decline to be ignored.

John Low, Golf Architect

Many men owe the grandeur of their lives to their tremendous difficulties.

Charles H. Spurgeon

Every golfer can expect to have four bad shots a round. When you do, just put them out of your mind.

Walter Hagen

You are meant to play the ball as it lies, a fact that may help to touch on your own objective approach to life.

Grantland Rice

The little troubles and worries of life, so many of which we meet, may be a stumbling block in our way, or we may make them stepping-stones to a noble character and to Heaven. Troubles are often the tools by which God fashions us for better things.

Henry Ward Beecher

Take your lies as they come.
Take the bad bounces with the good ones.

Ben Crenshaw

Kites rise highest against the wind, not with it.

Winston Churchill

Golf without bunkers and hazards would be tame and monotonous. So would life.

B. C. Forbes

A righteous man may have many troubles, but the Lord delivers him from them all.

Psalm 34:19

If there were no bunkers or hazards or impediments, the game of golf would be stripped of all interest and fascination.

W. T. Linskill

Acceptance of what has happened is the first step to overcoming the consequences of any misfortune.

William James

When in trouble, play the shot you know you can play, not the shot you hope you can play.

Jack Burke, Jr.

GOLF IS A FIVE-MILE WALK PUNCTUATED BY DISAPPOINTMENTS

The Cardinal
Bunker at
Prestwick Golf
Club, Scotland

ST. ANDREWS: THE HOME OF GOLF

In a book about Golf no apology is required for introducing some remarks on St. Andrews. Golf without St. Andrews would be almost as intolerable as St. Andrews without Golf. For here are the headquarters of the royal, ancient sport. Here Tom Morris holds his court; his courtiers, the clubmen and the caddies; his throne, the evergreen links; and his sceptre, a venerable putter. Here the children make their entrance into the world, not with silver spoons in their mouths, but with diminutive golf-clubs in their hands. Here the Champion is as much a hero as the greatest general who ever returned in triumph from the wars. Here is an asylum for golfing maniacs and the happy hunting-ground of the duffer, who, armed with a rusty cleek, sallies forth to mutilate the harmless turf.

> I have already said hundreds of times that I like it (St. Andrews) better than any golf course I have ever played and although I have played it many, many times, its charm for me increases with every round.
>
> Bobby Jones

Unidentified players, 1880

Here, there, and everywhere Golf is spreading: almost every day we hear of Tom Morris opening a new green and declaring it (with a faithless regularity) to be "the finest green in the country." Occasionally, he will modify the statement to this extent, that it is "second only to St. Andrews."

There are links which are sporting, and links which are long; links which have good putting greens, and links which have none at all; links which have no hazards, and links which are all hazard. But place any of them beside St. Andrews, and—oh, the difference! In short, St. Andrews is the home and nursery of Golf.

In St. Andrews are the hopes of the golfer fixed. The very air seems to be filled with the spirit of the game. At the tee with the brave old towers behind, the rolling waters of the Bay to the right, and in front the mounds, and hillocks, and levels of the links, one feels that he has reached the end of his pilgrimage to the Shrine of Golf. A new glamour is thrown about the game. He may foozle on the green under the critical eye of a by-standing professional, but "his heart's his own, his will is free." And standing at the end hole with his round half accomplished, he can survey the towers of the ruined Cathedral and the ragged masonry of the Castle, and the grey old city itself with the feeling of one who has found life worth living and Golf a game for men.

Robert Barclay, 1892

It may be truly said of St. Andrews that no portion of ground of the same size on the whole surface of the globe has afforded so much innocent enjoyment to so many people of all ages, and during so many generations.

A.J. Balfour, 1887, Golfer and British Prime Minister

The reason the Road Hole is the greatest par four in the world is because it's a par five.

Ben Crenshaw

The "Old" Course

As a boy growing up, Sam Snead was given some old iron clubheads made by Tom Stewart of St. Andrews. Loving sports, Sam cut down buggy whips for shafts and began beating balls around the cow pasture. He never expected anything to come of it. However in 1946, Sam found himself on the train from Edinburgh to St. Andrews to play the first Open following the war. Looking out the window, he thought he saw an old, run-down golf course. The boundary fences were falling down and the bunkers were in terrible shape. He asked a Scotsman beside him on the train, "What is that? It looks like an old, abandoned golf course." The Scotsman proudly sat up and replied, "It's the Old Course, home of the Royal and Ancient."

In spite of his surprise at the condition of the course, Snead won the Open that year and the $600 first prize. However, his expenses for the trip were $2700. Besides driving well, Sam's putting was superb that week as he used his Tom Stewart blade putter (which he had recently purchased) made in St. Andrews many years before.

British Open Champions
at St. Andrews

1873	Tom Kidd
1876	Bob Martin
1879	Jamie Anderson
1882	Bob Ferguson
1885	Bob Martin
1888	Jack Burns
1891	Hugh Kirkaldy
1895	J. H. Taylor
1900	J. H. Taylor
1905	James Braid
1910	James Braid
1921	Jock Hutchinson
1927	Robert T. Jones Jr.
1933	Denny Shute
1939	Richard Burton
1946	Sam Snead
1955	Peter Thomson
1957	Bobby Locke
1960	Kel Nagle
1964	Tony Lema
1970	Jack Nicklaus
1978	Jack Nicklaus
1984	Seve Ballesteros
1990	Nick Faldo
1995	John Daly

ONE STROKE AT A TIME—SECRETS OF GOLF & LIFE

It is nothing new or original to say that golf is played one stroke at a time. But it took me years to realize it.

Bobby Jones

When practicing, use the club that gives you the most trouble, not the one that gives you the most satisfaction.

Harry Vardon

Plunge boldly into the things of life!
Each lives it, not to many is it known;
and seize it where you will, it is interesting.

Johann Wolfgang von Goethe

Be a life long or short, its completeness depends on what it was lived for.

David Starr Jordan

Our aim should be service, not success.

Anonymous

The ability to convert visions to things is the secret of success.

Henry Ward Beecher

In golf as in life it's the follow-through that makes the difference.

Anonymous

The game of golf is not as easy as it seems. In the first place, the terrible inertia of the ball must be overcome.
Lord Wellwood, 1895

Competitive golf is played mainly on a five-and-a-half-inch course, the space between your ears.
Bobby Jones

Perhaps the dominant force in the average life is possessions. Life becomes a scramble for gain instead of a mission for God. We are so busy making a living that we forget to make a life.

A. P. Gouthey

The meaning of earthly existence lies, not as we have grown used to thinking, in prospering, but in the development of the soul.

Alexander Solzhenitsyn

To control his own ball, all alone without help or hindrance, the golfer must first and last control himself. At each stroke, the ball becomes a vital extension, an image of one's innermost self.

John Stuart Martin

Do not wear yourself out to get rich; have the wisdom to show restraint. Cast but a glance at riches, and they are gone.

Proverbs 23:4-5

You must work very hard to become a natural golfer.

Gary Player

We cannot do everything at once, but we must do something at once

Calvin Coolidge

Correct one fault at a time. Concentrate on the one fault you want to overcome.

Sam Snead

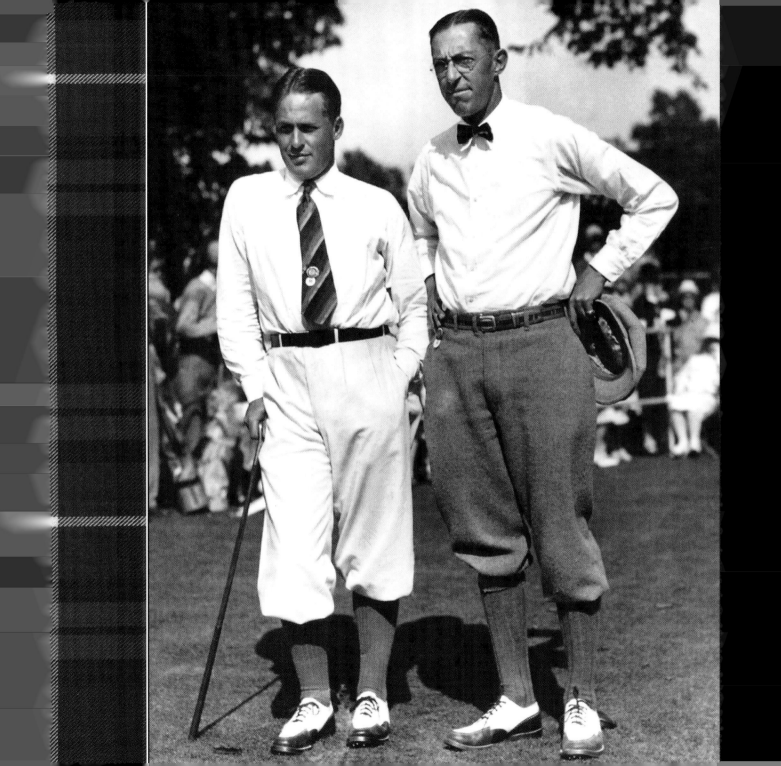

NEVER GIVE UP

No golfer ever personified perseverance and gritty determination better than Ben Hogan. Showing little natural talent and dropping off the tour twice by 1934, Ben refused to quit. With aching hands, he practiced daily for three years and returned in 1937 for good. In 1948, he won his first U.S. Open and ten other tournaments. Then on a foggy February morning in 1949, a speeding bus crossed over in front of him on the highway nearly killing him and his wife, Valerie. His pelvis, collarbone, numerous ribs and an ankle were broken. Again refusing to give up, Ben returned in 1950 not only to play, but to win. That summer at Merion, he won his second of four U.S. Opens. With his legs heavily bandaged, in unbearable pain and hardly able to walk, by sheer force of will Ben managed to rally, force a playoff, and to win. No other golfer in America could have done it.

No matter what happens—never give up a hole.
In tossing in your cards after a bad beginning you also undermine your whole game, because to quit between tee and green is more habit-forming than drinking a highball before breakfast.

Sam Snead

The real test of golf and of life is not keeping out of the rough, but getting out after we are in.

Anonymous

Don't let the bad shots get to you. Don't let yourself become angry. The true scramblers are thick-skinned. And they always beat the whiners.

Paul Runyan

Nothing in the world can take the place of persistence. Talent will not; nothing is more common than unsuccessful men with talent. Genius will not; unrewarded genius is almost a proverb. Education will not; the world is full of educated derelicts. Persistence and determination alone are omnipotent. The slogan "press on!" has solved and always will solve the problems of the human race.

Calvin Coolidge

You never really lose until you quit trying.

Mike Ditka

No matter what happens, keep on hitting the ball.

Harry Vardon

My philosophy? Practice, practice, practice — and win.

Babe Didrikson Zaharias

Don't be discouraged; everyone who got where he is, started where he was.

Anonymous

Nothing in the world can take the place of persistence. The greatest mistake is giving up.

Anonymous

Golf is a game of finding what works, losing it, and finding it again.

Ken Venturi

Never, never, never, never give up.
Winston Churchill

There is no failure except in no longer trying.
Anonymous

Dr. Laidlow Purves (putting) and Arthur Molesworth playing on the Wimbledon Commons. As evident by the grazing sheep, the Commons was a public park and not exclusively devoted to golf. All early courses were as such.

There are no shortcuts to any place worth going.

Source Unknown

Perseverance is a great element of success. If you only knock long enough and loud enough at the gate, you are sure to wake up somebody.

Henry Wadsworth Longfellow

Success seems to be largely a matter of hanging on after others have let go.

William Feather

Forgetting what is behind and straining toward what is ahead, I press on toward the goal to win the prize for which God has called me heavenward.

Philippians 3:13-14

The price and the glory of a mortal's life is that "we never arrive; we are always on the way."

D. Elton Trueblood

PRESIDENTIAL STROKES

W hile Dwight Eisenhower and Gerald Ford may be noted as America's premier golfing presidents, William Howard Taft was the first president to vigorously embrace golf and to be frequently photographed playing the game.

Within a few years of the establishment of the first golf club in America in 1888, golf quickly captured the hearts and lives of thousands of Americans. Soon the country would have more than 200 golf courses—more than the rest of the world combined. Golf represented the "good life" in the carefree days prior to World War I.

Recently elected in 1908, President William Howard Taft was an avid golfer and the model for aspiring businessmen and politicians. As the featured speaker for the 20th Anniversary Dinner of the St. Andrew's Golf Club of Yonkers, New York, he said:

> When I heard that your club—the oldest in the country—is only 20 years old, and realize that I have been playing golf since 1896, I am surprised. I would, in respect to any other matter, feel very much discouraged at having attained in so long a time so little excellence. But golf is different from other games. Pope's lines have a greater application to it than to any other sport I know: "Hope springs eternal in the human breast; Man never is, but always will be, blest."

And while Taft's popularity has waned over the century, presidential golf has not.

President William Howard Taft playing the Provincetown course on Cape Cod

I know I'm getting better at golf because I'm hitting fewer spectators.
Gerald Ford

As President, Dwight Eisenhower had the USGA help install a putting green on the South Lawn of the White House, played golf nearly every Wednesday at Burning Tree, and attended the Masters every year. However, the happiest day of his golf career came on February 6, 1968, in Palm Springs. On that day, at the age of 77, he hit his one and only hole-in-one.

A FEW GOOD LAUGHS

Shortly after the game itself was invented, a Scottish pundit invented the first joke of golf. At the time, it was mildly amusing.

Since then, it has been told and retold with regional and even historical nuances. Every golfer has heard at least 13 variations of it. Every pub within a thousand yards of a golf course has banned it, and it should be banned in polite golf society for all times. However, just for the younger players, here it is for the *last time*:

> *Once in Scotland I played with the most fanatical golfer I've ever met. We were just teeing off on the 15th where the green lies next to the main road. He was in the middle of his backswing when a row of funeral cars came past. He stopped, took off his cap, held it over his heart and bowed his head. I was impressed. I said, "You're a man who shows real respect for the deceased." He said, "It's only fair. If she had lived until next Tuesday, we would have been married 37 years."*

Keep your sense of humor. There's enough stress in the rest of your life to let bad shots ruin a game you're supposed to enjoy.

Amy Alcott

A person rarely succeeds at anything unless he has fun doing it.

Anonymous

We are all here for a spell, get all the good laughs you can.

Will Rogers

You don't stop laughing because you grow old, you grow old because you stop laughing.

Anonymous

Blessed is he who has learned to laugh at himself, for he shall never cease to be entertained.

John Boswell

At least he can't cheat on his score—because all you have to do is look back down the fairway and count the wounded.

Bob Hope

A cheerful heart is good medicine, but a crushed spirit dries up the bones.

Proverbs 17:22

I was three over: one over a house, one over a patio, and one over a swimming pool.

George Brett

An avid golfer died and was carried to heaven. He discovered it to be a magnificent golf course flanked by trees, a celestial Pinehurst or Augusta. Setting out to explore the heavenly course with his angel guide, he saw a player attempting to cut the corner of a dog leg, a feat demanding a carry of at least 300 yards.

"That shot will be a miracle," commented the newcomer. "Who does he think he is — St. Peter?"

"Well, it *is* St. Peter," whispered the angel, "but he *thinks* he's Arnold Palmer."

My swing is so bad I look like a caveman killing his lunch.
Lee Trevino

The fairways were so narrow you had to walk down them single file.
Sam Snead

THE TRUE MEANING OF SUCCESS

T he most important thing is to have people feel that I've been reliable and I've been good for the game of golf as well as a good citizen.

Byron Nelson

Success is reached by being active, awake, ahead of the crowd, by aiming high, pushing ahead, honestly, diligently, patiently; by climbing, digging, saving; by forgetting the past, using the present, trusting in the future; by honoring God, having a purpose, fainting not, determining to win, and striving to the end.

Russell Conwell

The purpose of life is to serve and to show compassion and the will to help others. Only then have we ourselves become true human beings.

Albert Schweitzer

The longer I live the more I am convinced that the one thing worth living for and dying for is the privilege of making someone more happy and more useful. No man who ever does anything to lift his fellows ever makes a sacrifice.

Booker T. Washington

It's not true that nice guys finish last. Nice guys are winners before the game even starts.

Addison Walker

Blessed is he who has regard for the weak; the Lord delivers him in times of trouble. The Lord will protect him and preserve his life; he will bless him in the land.

Psalm 41:1-2

Some persons think they have made a success of life when all they have made is money.

Anonymous

Live for something. Do good and leave behind you a monument of virtue, which the storms of time can never destroy. Write your name in kindness, love, and mercy on the hearts of those who come in contact with you, and you will never be forgotten.

Thomas Chalmers

Successful competitors want to win. Head cases want to win at all costs.

Nancy Lopez

The two hardest things to handle in life are failure and success.

Unknown

Success now means far more than mere money-getting. A broad general definition of success may be summarized as follows: The ability to be self-sustaining, the practice of making others happy, the ability to win and hold the respect of society, and joy just in being alive.

A. B. Zu Tavern

It is wise to keep in mind that neither success nor failure is ever final.

Roger Babson

There are two things to aim at in life: first, to get what you want; and, after that, to enjoy it. Only the wisest achieve the second.

Logan Pearsall Smith

Success is not measured by the money earned but by the service rendered.

Roy L. Smith

LEAVE BEHIND YOU A MONUMENT OF VIRTUE

MAY I CARRY YOUR BAG?

"C ads," "cawds," or "cadies" were originally itinerant messengers of all ages particularly around Edinburgh who delivered messages and parcels. So it was only natural that these young boys and older men added the carrying of golf clubs to their duties.

With the increased interest in golf, carrying clubs for a fee became more popular and profitable. But "caddies," as they came to be called, were still living on bare essentials.

"Old Da" Anderson, a former caddie, served up tasty refreshments and colorful golf stories on the fourth hole at St. Andrews.

They were known for wearing ill-fitting, castoff clothes from their golf patrons and cumbersome boots or going barefooted. Caddies often attached themselves to men of similar size and build so that the hand-me-down clothes would be a better fit. As a result, the affluent golfer and the poorer caddie soon came to look alike and even to develop strong friendships in Scotland's classless society. At St. Andrews, a caddie once commented to a visiting golfer that he had carried for Prime Minister Balfour and that the two were close acquaintances. The amused golfer did not believe the caddie and asked what he meant by "close acquaintance." The caddie quickly replied, "Joast this. I am weering a pair o' Mr. Balfour's troosers!"

During the 19th century, different types of caddies developed. The carrying caddie was the senior and more experienced. He not only carried clubs but gave advice along the course to new players. The other, the forecaddie, was ahead of the golfer to see where the ball went. Forecaddies were both "fixed" in one spot and "moving" as the ball advanced. Forecaddies were more necessary then because of the many blind holes and the number of people walking across the public grounds being used for golf.

When the golfer had hit a particularly long or errant shot and the forecaddie was in danger of being hit, he would yell "Forecaddie!" to warn him. While the role of the forecaddie disappeared, the warning endured and became the familiar "fore" used today.

The carrying caddie also made sand tees from the sand box near each tee area and tried to give his player every advantage. At first he carried clubs loosely in his arms, but that would change. A former sailor and sailmaker made a few narrow canvas bags for the clubs. Initially the caddies refused to use them, carrying the bag in one arm and the loose clubs in the other. But common sense eventually prevailed over blind tradition. A shoulder strap was later added and the golf bag was created.

Today's mature professional caddie little resembles the youthful lad or old man in hand-me-down clothes of the past. For example, Tip Anderson first caddied for Arnold Palmer in 1960 at the Open in St. Andrews and became Arnold's exclusive caddie for tournaments in Scotland and England. They were quite a team. A career caddie, Anderson is now a celebrity and the most requested caddie in St. Andrews. As he said, "Forgive my lack of modesty, but I am the most experienced and best regular caddie at the Old Course at St. Andrews. I have caddied there at least four times a week for the last 44 years, since I was 14 years old."

Two Shillings and a Lunch

My first job was a forecaddie, and I daresay it would be a couple of years before I was promoted to a carrying caddie. We used to get two shillings per day when acting as forecaddie with a lunch at Mrs. Forman's consisting of fourpence worth of bread and cheese. Those were happy days!

Anonymous Musselburgh Caddie

If you can smile when all around you have lost their heads — you must be the caddie.
Anonymous

If I needed advice from my caddie, he'd be hitting the shots and I'd be carrying the bag.
Bobby Jones

LIVING ON THE EDGE

A positive attitude is always the mental edge that separates great players from good players. We must continually ignore and shield ourselves from negative comments—even from those who love us. Clara Hogan, Ben's mother, often told him as a teenager, "You'll never get anywhere fooling around those golf courses." Fortunately, Ben was able to overcome those comments. Most of us would not have.

Vigilantly guard your mind against erroneous and destructive thought as you would guard your house against burglars and assassins.

Grenville Kleiser

You talk to yourself all the time, be careful what you say. Negative images are destructive.

William Lantz

A bad attitude is worse than a bad swing.

Payne Stewart

As a man thinks in his heart so is he.

Proverbs 23:7

The first thing anybody has to do to be any good at anything is to believe in himself.

Gay Brewer

To control your nerves, you must have a positive thought in your mind.

Byron Nelson

They can conquer who believe they can.

Ralph Waldo Emerson

The difference between winning and losing is always a mental one.

Peter Thomson

Never tell yourself you can't make a shot. Remember, we are what we think we are.

Gary Player

To be good company for ourselves we must store our minds well, fill them with happy and pure thought, with pleasant memories of the past, and reasonable hopes of the future.

John Lubbock

Success or failure in business is caused more by mental attitude than by mental capacities.

Walter Dill Scott

If there is a doubt in your mind over a golf shot, how can your muscles know what they are expected to do?

Harvey Penick

Always look out for the sunlight the Lord sends into your days.

Hope Campbell

Optimism doesn't wait on facts. It deals with prospects. Pessimism is a waste of time.

Norman Cousins

You are what you think you are, in golf and in life.
Raymond Floyd

The greatest single lesson to be learned from golf is mental discipline.
Louise Suggs
U.S. Women's Open
Champion 1949 & 1952

It is said that Arnold Palmer has a lone framed plaque on his office wall that explains his success on and off the golf course. It reads:

If you think you are beaten, you are.
If you think you dare not, you don't.
If you like to win but think you can't,
It's almost certain that you won't.

Life's battles don't always go
To the stronger woman or man,
But soon or later, those who win
Are those who think they can.

The game of golf is 90 percent mental and ten percent mental.

Anonymous

We create success or failure on the course primarily by our thoughts.

Gary Player

I don't dwell on bad shots, bad rounds, or bad tournaments. I don't play in the past. I play in the present.

Raymond Floyd

Given an equality of strength and skill, the victory in golf will be to him who is captain of his soul.

Arnold Haultain

Golf is a matter of confidence. If you think you cannot do it, there is no chance you will.

Henry Cotton

The world is full of cactus, but we don't have to sit on it.

Anonymous

Every man has enough power left to carry out that of which he is fully convinced.

Johann Wolfgang von Goethe

Golfers were required to wear a red coat because golf was originally played on the town commons—the public park open to all for walking, grazing sheep, or hanging laundry. The red coat alerted the unsuspecting public of the approaching danger of being hit by a flying white ball.

BRITAIN'S ROYALTY OF GOLF

Three British professionals so totally dominated golf from 1894 to 1914 that they came to be known as The Great Triumvirate. In addition to many other tournaments, among them they won 16 British Open Championships and placed second in it 12 times during a 21-year period.

JOHN HENRY TAYLOR was the youngest of the three, but was the first to gain golfing notoriety. A natural speaker and gifted leader, he would have made his mark in any walk of life. He won the Open five times with a flat-footed swing and monotonously boring straight drives. According to Bernard Darwin, "When he pulled down his cap, stuck out his chin, and embedded those large boots in the ground, he could hit straight through the wind as if it were not there." He did not win every championship, but when he did win, he won easily.

HARRY VARDON, the only man to have won the British Open six times, did so when it was the premier event in the world of golf. The first four victories were in 1896, 1898, 1899, and 1903. Later, after two major bouts with tuberculosis, Harry won his fifth and sixth Open in 1911 and 1914. Using only seven clubs, Vardon's hands were extremely large and his fingers were described as a "bunch of sausages wrapped around a baton." Gene Sarazen said that Vardon was "the epitome of confidence. Often, he would play a shot and then replace his divot before bothering to see where the ball had gone. He didn't have to see. He knew."

JAMES BRAID won the Open five times in nine years. His unorthodox style was not exactly "graceful," but his undeniable eye and muscle coordination gave him a concentration and power that were always under control. Horace Hutchinson thought Braid's lack of grace made him particularly fascinating to watch. As Hutchinson was to say later, "This sounds a paradox; but there is a special delight in seeing the kind of divine fury with which he 'laces into' the ball, and yet the wonderful accuracy with which the club meets the ball."

By all the good golfing qualities of courage and sticking power and chivalry, by their modesty and dignity and self-respect, they helped to make the professional golfer a very different person from what he was when they first came on the scene. Their influence as human beings has been as remarkable as their achievements as golfers.

Bernard Darwin
British Golf Writer, 1930

I consider putting, next to the mashie approach, the most important stroke in golf. I always carry two different kinds of putters and I have several different stances, and if I am off with one putter I try the other and keep altering my stance until I feel perfectly comfortable; for without this feeling you cannot have confidence, and without confidence good and accurate putting is an impossibility.

Harry Vardon

PUTTING... THE MOST IMPORTANT STROKE IN GOLFING

Keep on hitting it straight until the wee ball goes in the hole.
James Braid

Golfers find it a very trying matter to turn at the waist, more particularly if they have a lot of waist to turn.
Harry Vardon

This, the most famous golf picture of all time, shows Harry Vardon driving off the second tee of the Old Course at St. Andrews. Painted by Clement Flower in 1913.

ROYAL SPORT OR ANCIENT ADDICTION?

Golf is not a mere game. It is a disease, infectious and contagious, which once acquired cannot be shaken off. Once a golfer always a golfer—there's no help for it!

The game exercises a spell, a thrall over the man who has once swung a club. You begin casually and experimentally. A golfing friend hands you a driving iron and asks you to have a "whang" at a golf ball. Well, you "whang" and your fate is sealed. You are a golfer from that moment. Most likely you missed the ball and you mutter between your teeth that you'll go on whanging till you knock that ball into the next field. Or you, by the extreme chance (as you discover later), give the ball a fine swinging smack and to your delight see the lively bit of white soaring in the air to drop a full hundred yards off.

> GOLF IS NOT A MERE GAME. IT IS A DISEASE

Then with a mild chuckle you hand back your friend his iron and exultantly observe that you think this game would "suit you" thoroughly. Whatever your luck—whether you hit or whether you missed—you are a golf-infected person. The incipient stages of the disease are rapid. You buy a set of clubs, clandestinely and ill-advisedly, seeking no advice, and probably acquiring tools which indeed prove "ill adapted for putting the little balls into the little holes." Then you sally forth covertly to practice and to fret away your soul in vain endeavours to "drive." You practice "putting"—which looks so easy, but is so tricky you fume and perspire at your own ineptitude.

L. Latchford, 1903

Golf is a terrible, hopeless addiction, it seems. It makes its devotees willing to trudge miles in any manner of weather, lugging a huge, incommodious and appallingly heavy bag with them, in pursuit of a tiny and fantastically expensive ball, in a fanatical attempt to direct it into a hole the size of a beer glass half a mile away. If anything could be better calculated to convince one of the essential lunacy of the human race, I haven't found it.

Mike Seabrook

Never the sort of person who could be content to do anything badly, Bob Coyne had applied himself to the Royal and Ancient Pastime with all the simple earnestness and dogged determination of a silent, self-centered man. He had taken lessons from the professional. He had brought his driver home and practiced with it in the backyard. He had read books on the subject. He had studied the methods and styles of the best players. He had formed theories of his own as to stance and swing. He had even talked golf to his wife—which is the last stage of incurable golfitis.

Charles Van Loan

I'm a golfaholic, no question about that. Counseling wouldn't help me. They'd have to put me in prison, and then I'd talk the warden into building a hole or two and teach him how to play.

Lee Trevino

The ardent golfer would play Mount Everest if somebody would put a flagstick on top.
Pete Dye

Golf is an ideal diversion, but a ruinous disease.
Bertie Charles Forbes

Surviving British Open Champions, St. Andrews, 1905

When Jerry West was asked how many days a week he played golf, he replied, "Only on days ending in Y."

My conscience hurt me. I hate to play golf when I should be out working, so the only thing to do was quit working.

Jim Umbracht

After an abominable round of golf, a man is known to have slit his wrists with a razor blade, and, having bandaged them, to have stumbled into the locker room and enquired of his partner, "What time tomorrow?"

Alistair Cooke

Alexander McKellar was probably the most addicted golfer to ever play the game. Spending the entire day at Bruntsfield Links in Edinburgh, he practiced at night by lamplight. He played year 'round—even in the snow if it was frozen hard enough. This fanatical devotion finally drove his wife to despair. In a satirical effort to shame him and point out the extent of his addiction, one night she carried his dinner and nightcap to him on the course. Failing to see the ridiculousness of it all and engrossed in his game, Alexander told her he did not have time to stop for dinner.

THE AMATEUR CHAMPIONSHIP IN AMERICA

H. L. Fitzpatrick was the "First American Golf Writer" and covered the early game in person. However, newspapers did not know how or where to print golfing news. What was golf? Was it a social event or a sport?

The United States golf contests began only in 1894, and then were really the outcome of a zealous disagreement. The golfing fever was just changing from calm to quick, and both the Newport Golf Club and the St. Andrew's Golf Club (Yonkers, NY) determined to hold championship tournaments.

And so in the last week of August, when the social season was at its height in Newport, some 30 golfers met at medal play over a short but well-planned course. None of our home-bred players were in the finals, for the winner was William Lawrence who had learned the game at Pau, France. The second finisher, C. B. Macdonald, learned his golf while a student at St. Andrews University, Scotland's famed mecca for golfers.

The following tournament at St. Andrews was a more pretentious one with the winner of the gold-and-diamond badge (L. B. Stoddart) proclaimed the "Amateur Champion of the United States."

In view of the conflict between the two rival clubs and champions, it could not be said that the amateur championship had been satisfactorily settled. The disagreement regarding the respective value and importance of our two championship meetings made it evident that there was need of some permanent body to guide the affairs of the game. The result was the creation of the United States Golf Association at a meeting in New York on December 24, 1894. The five clubs represented at the first meeting were the nucleus of a society now containing nearly 200 clubs as associate and allied members. The first amateur championship under the new order of things was held at Newport in October 1895. The late date was chosen to avoid a conflict with international yacht races.

On the first day, 32 players left the first tee and included doctors, lawyers, clergymen, and men of business prominence. College players had not yet developed into championship form and did not attend. A fine crop of club champions had mustered together for this competition, but the finals narrowed down to a match between Macdonald and Charles E. Sands, a lawn tennis player of repute, who had been at golf for only some three months. Good luck brought him to the finals, much to his surprise.

Sands had foozled his drive from the first tee in every match of the week, and he did the same in starting out with Macdonald who won by 12 up and 11 to play.

Macdonald's reign as champion lasted until July 1896, when the amateurs met on the sand dunes at Southampton. At last they had an 18-hole course to play over, although the Shinnecock Hills Golf Club links then measured only 4,423 yards in playing distances and would now be termed a short course. H. J. Whigham won the second championship with his wooden putter and was the sensation of the meeting. Few of our players had ever seen a wooden putter, and to run up an approach instead of pitching up had been considered "bad form." It was croquet, not golf.

As at Newport, the life at the Shinnecock Hills Golf Club ended each day with the posting up of the scores, and there was a constant round of dances and dinners at the country houses during the week.

H. L. Fitzpatrick, 1898, the "First American Golf Writer"

The early game in America was dominated by amateurs and by men who had learned their game in Britain.

Notable U.S. Amateur Champions

Francis Quimet (1914, 1931)

Bobby Jones (1924, 1925, 1927, 1928, 1930)

Gene Littler (1953)

Arnold Palmer (1954)

Jack Nicklaus (1959, 1961)

Lanny Wadkins (1970)

Craig Stadler (1973)

Mark O'Meara (1979)

Hal Sutton (1980)

Tiger Woods (1994, 1995, 1996)

Theodore A. Havemeyer presents the first USGA trophy to Charles Blair Macdonald for his Amateur Championship victory in 1895. Macdonald was a competent golfer, but was to be best known as a course designer or "golf architect" as he called it. His son-in-law, H. J. Whigham, won the trophy in 1896 and 1897.

HUMBLING EXPERIENCES

Life, like golf, can be humbling. However, little good comes from brooding about mistakes we've made. The next shot, in golf or in life, is the big one.

Grantland Rice
Writer, Golfer, and Friend of Bobby Jones

Great tranquillity of heart is he who cares for neither praise nor blame.

Thomas à Kempis

Glenna Collett Vare, winner of six U.S. Women's Amateur Championships, shown with her first trophy in 1922. She was the preeminent woman player of the 1920s.

Humility grows out of strength. Pride grows out of weakness.
Anonymous

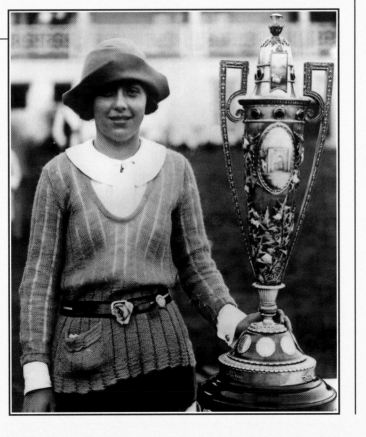

I believe the first test of a truly great man is his humility.

John Ruskin

Golf acts as a corrective against sinful pride. I attribute the insane arrogance of the later Roman emperors almost entirely to the fact that, never having played golf, they never knew that strange chastening humility which is engendered by a topped chip shot.

P. G. Wodehouse

Humility and the fear of the Lord bring wealth and honor and life.

Proverbs 22:4

In golf, humiliations are the essence of the game.

Alistair Cooke

The man who thinks too much of himself usually thinks too little of others.

Anonymous

Be brave if you lose and meek if you win.

Harvey Penick

What makes humility so desirable is the marvelous thing it does to us; it creates in us a capacity for the closest possible intimacy with God.

M. Baldwin

A great man is always willing to be little.

Ralph Waldo Emerson

THE PGA: BEGINNINGS AND EARLY DAYS

In 1916, Rodman Wanamaker (the Philadelphia department store heir) conceived of a tournament for professional golfers only and the PGA Championship was created. While only 31 players came, the $2,500 purse was truly significant for its day and was won by Jim Barnes. Wanamaker knew that golf had long been the domain of the amateur, but he foresaw that the future belonged to the professionals.

In Britain, the class system kept the amateur golfer in control for another ten years or more, but in America, professional golf began its run at clear superiority. During the 1920s, Walter Hagen dominated the PGA, combining golf and showmanship with a flair for the expensive and dramatic. The only distraction to Hagen's victories was that Bobby Jones (an amateur) was still the best golfer in America. In 1922, Hagen was the first American to win the British Open—a feat now considered routine—and established the equality of American and British golf. After the amateurs Francis Quimet and Bobby Jones retired, professionals would take control of golf for good.

The pro tour as such was still years in the making. A few winter resorts in California, Texas, and Florida paid players to put on exhibitions or tournaments, but the money was not enough to live on. Even the best players like

Jimmy Demaret and Byron Nelson had to keep their jobs as club pros while taking time off to play in a few tournaments each year. Golfers drove cross-country together in old cars, staying in "modest" accommodations and skimping on meals just for the opportunity to play and to compete for the small cash prizes.

In 1936, the tour purses totaled about $100,000. The leading money winner, Horton Smith, earned $7,682 for his efforts. This early, adolescent version of the PGA was nothing like the modern megabusiness it is now.

PGA tour purses passed the $1 million mark in 1958 for the first time. In 1963, Arnold Palmer became the first golfer to win more than $100,000 in one year. Curtis Strange was the first golfer to win more than $1 million in one year, 1988.

Golf is not your life, it's not your wife, it's only a game.
Lloyd Mangrum

PLAYING BY THE RULES

Good sportsmanship is the essence of golf, and no one exemplified that more than Bobby Jones. In the 1925 U.S. Open, Jones's ball moved when he addressed it. No one else had seen it move, so Jones called the penalty on himself. That penalty ended up costing him the championship. "There's only one way to play the game," he said when later asked about it. "You might as well praise a man for not robbing a bank as to praise him for playing by the rules."

I didn't think of the tour as something glamorous. I just wanted to play to beat somebody. My parents didn't know much about golf, but they gave me their blessing. They said, "Be a good man and do right."

Byron Nelson

There is no game which teaches honesty to the same extent as golf. There is no referee, and the rules are based on the assumption that every golfer is strictly honest. What other game depends on the integrity of the player to such an extent, that even if he is out in the rough, alone with his Maker, and loses a stroke because his ball rolls over in addressing it, he must at once acquaint his opponent with the penalty?

Alister MacKenzie

I hope I shall always possess firmness and virtue enough to maintain what I consider the most amiable of all titles, the character of an honest man.

George Washington

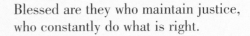

Blessed are they who maintain justice, who constantly do what is right.

Psalm 106:3

Always do right. This will surprise some people and astonish the rest.

Mark Twain

To be persuasive, we must be believable.
To be believable, we must be credible.
To be credible, we must be truthful.

Edward R. Murrow

There are two things the players on tours should realize: Adults will copy your swing, and young people will follow your example.

Harvey Penick

The greatest man is he who chooses the right with invincible resolution, who resists the sorest temptations from within and without, who bears the heaviest burdens cheerfully, who is calmest in storms and most fearless under menace and frowns, and whose reliance on truth, virtue, and on God is most unfaltering.

William Ellery Channing

Golf liars have one advantage over the fishing kind—they don't have to show anything to prove it.

Anonymous

Honesty is after all the basic starting point of character. Honesty is the indispensable essential of every worthwhile success.

Charles Gow

There's only one way to play the game. You might as well praise a man for not robbing a bank as to praise him for playing by the rules.

Bobby Jones

In the autumn of 1930, with no more worlds to conquer, Bobby Jones the Atlanta barrister decided to put away his famous "Calamity Jane" that had done such devastating work, along with the rest of his golfing weapons and call it a day.

H.B. Martin

NO PERFECT GOLFERS

The game of golf is a game of accepting failure; of accepting imperfection; of realizing that the perfect game has never been played, never will be played, or ever could be played.

Anonymous

Don't let what you cannot do interfere with what you can do.

Anonymous

Do what you can, with what you have, where you are.

Theodore Roosevelt

He is a wise man who does not grieve for the things which he has not, but rejoices for those which he has.

Epictetus

Golf is a game of mistakes, and the object is to keep your bad shots straight and in play.

Ben Hogan

I have learned the secret of being content in any and every situation.

Philippians 4:12

Charles Blair Macdonald, shown striking the ball, learned his golf from Old Tom Morris while a student at St. Andrews.

Golf is not a game of great shots. It's a game of the most accurate misses.

Gene Littler

TREACHEROUS LIES

In a devious and treacherous effort to harm the game, a great many shameless and bald-faced lies have been told about the ancient and royal pastime:

Golf is a game whose aim is to hit a very small ball into an even smaller hole, with weapons singularly ill-designed for the purpose.

Winston Churchill

If every golfer in the world, male and female, were laid end to end, I for one, would leave them there.

Mark Parkinson
President of the Anti-Golf Society

What earthly good is golf? Life is stern and life is earnest. We live in a practical age. All around us we see foreign competition making itself unpleasant. And we spend our time playing golf! What do we get out of it? Is golf any use? That's what I'm asking you. Can you name me a single case where devotion to this pestilential pastime has done a man any practical good?

P. G. Wodehouse

It's so ridiculous to see a golfer with a one-foot putt and everybody is saying "Shhh" and not moving a muscle. Then we allow 19-year-old kids to face a game-deciding free throw with 17,000 people yelling.

Al McGuire

There are three ways of learning golf: by study, which is the most wearisome; by imitation, which is the most fallacious; and by experience, which is the most bitter.

Robert Browning

A golf course is the epitome of all that is purely transitory in the universe, a space not to dwell in, but to get over as quickly as possible.

Jean Giraudoux

If you pick up a golfer and hold it close to your ear, like a conch shell, and listen, you will hear an alibi.

Fred Beck

There are three things that are as unfathomable as they are fascinating to the masculine mind: metaphysics, golf and the feminine heart.
Arnold Haultain

Ben and Byron at Augusta in 1946 before the final round

THE GLORIOUS SONS OF GLEN GARDEN

Walking into the clubhouse at Glen Garden Country Club in Fort Worth for the first time, visitors are amazed to discover the club's singular place in golf history: two former caddies are two of the greatest legends in the game.

When both boys were about 13, Byron Nelson and Ben Hogan became caddies at Glen Garden. From different schools and different neighborhoods, they gradually became acquainted during spare moments at the club. At Christmas of 1927, the club held its annual Caddie Championship, where Byron and Ben played together for the first time. Ben was a small, very quiet boy with big hands and strong arms, while Byron was already six feet two inches and playing hooky from school to play golf. Byron sank a long putt on the last hole of the tournament to tie Ben and force a playoff. Byron won by one shot. Little did they know history would repeat itself several more times.

In 1930, Ben turned pro and Byron in 1932. From the beginning, they were different in nearly every way. Byron took to the game easily, studying Harry Vardon's old book on golf and playing every chance he got. His famous grip was developed soon after he and the Scottish pro Bobby Cruikshank played together in the Texas Open Pro-Am. After the tournament, which they won, all Bobby said to Byron was, "Laddie, if ye don't larn to grip the club right, ye'll niver make a good player."

Ben, on the other hand, had a terrible hook and was slow to develop. He would stay on the tour for awhile, run out of money, drop out and return home for a number of times before he was there to stay. Ben's persistence, perseverance and dedication were evident in his long hours of practice.

This dedication to practice was soon to be a point of public discussion. Mirroring their first Christmas Caddie Tournament, Byron and Ben were tied at the end of regulation play for the 1940 Texas Open. It was here that Ben made his famous remark on the radio that afternoon about Byron's practice, or lack of it. He said, "Byron's got a good game, but it'd be a lot better if he'd practice. He's too lazy to practice." Not one to be offended, the next day Byron again won the playoff by one stroke. Commenting on his constant ability to beat his friend, Byron said, "It seems as if I played better against Ben on the average than I did against anybody else. I tried harder against him, because I knew I had to."

The next time the boy caddies would tie at the end of regulation play would be the 1942 Masters. Byron won again, in spite of being so nervous the night before that he slept little and threw up the next morning before they started. The most remarkable thing, though, was that all of the other pros stayed over to watch the historic playoff.

While Byron won two Masters, one U.S. Open and two PGA Championships, he is most remembered for "The Streak of 1945" in which he won 11 tournaments in a row and 18 for the year. Ben conquered a bad hook and a near fatal highway tragedy to win four U.S. Opens, two PGAs, two Masters and one British Open. Caddies, friends, competitors—Byron and Ben are the glorious sons of Glen Garden. No other club in America claims such a heritage.

> BYRON'S GOT A GOOD GAME, BUT... HE'S TOO LAZY TO PRACTICE

Winners are different. They're a different breed of cat.
Byron Nelson

This is a game of misses. The guy who misses the best is going to win.
Ben Hogan

THE PROMISE: HEALTH, HAPPINESS, & LONG LIFE

Out of a possible 75 millions (allowing for infants and infirm octogenarians), there are less than a million people in this country who play golf. At least 74 millions are wilfully depriving themselves of one of the most certain methods of attaining health and happiness. If you were assured that without imbibing any new-fangled religion and regardless of all the new dietists and doctors, you could not only add 20 years to the normal span of life, but secure at least one good day every week by the simple process of swinging a golf club, would you not rush to the nearest golf links and begin to take lessons from the local professional?

There really is no question about the results any more than there is about the pleasures of the game. Every other form of outdoor sport loses its attraction sooner or later. Baseball, football, riding, polo, even tennis abandon us or we abandon them as our wind gets shorter and our bones more brittle. But once a golfer, you are wedded to the game for life. Nearly all who ever played golf and gave it up are those to whom athletic exercise in any shape is abhorrent. A few—perhaps even more than a few—have attempted to learn the game and have renounced it in disgust. Either they could not see any fun in it or because they were such hopeless duffers that any sort of proficiency seemed out of the question.

These might well have been saved if they had only gone about it the right way. It is to these and to the many millions who have never even attempted to play that a few words of advice may be offered. If they will follow the advice given we guarantee health, sleep, immunity from nervous prostration and business worries, good temper, mental control, and lastly long life barring accidents from taxicabs or air ships.

H. J. Whigham, U.S. Amateur Champion, 1896 and 1897

*In golf,
as in life,
you get
what you
put into it.*
Sam Snead

*A well-adjusted
man is one
who can play
golf as if it
were a game.*
Anonymous